P9-DCI-931

THE NEW PLANT LIBRARY

# CLEMATIS

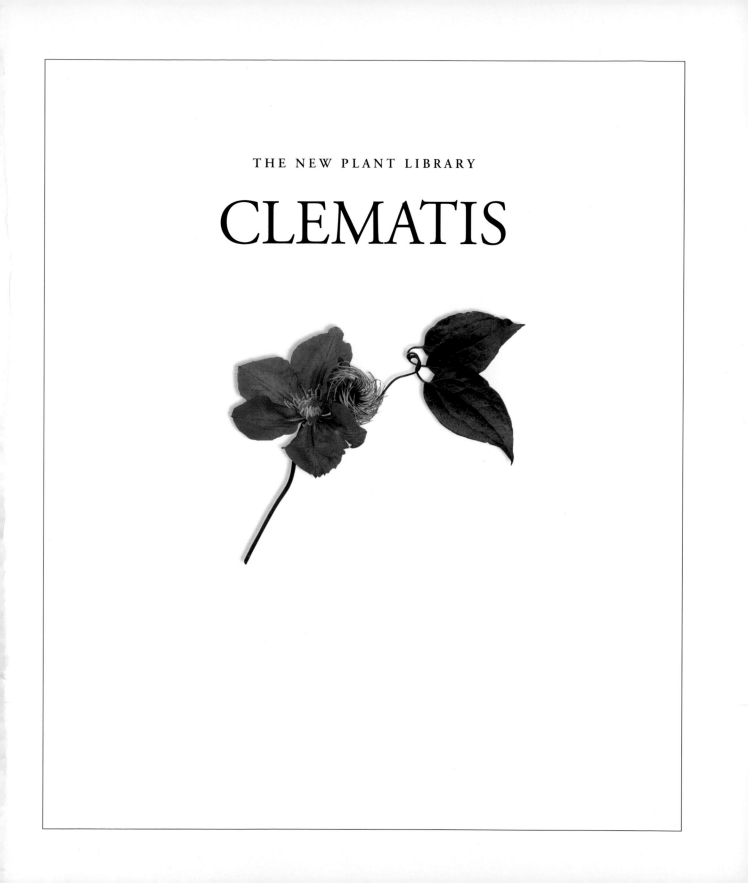

THE NEW PLANT LIBRARY

# CLEMATIS

ANDREW MIKOLAJSKI

Consultant: Christopher Grey-Wilson
Photography by Peter Anderson

LORENZ BOOKS
NEW YORK • LONDON • SYDNEY • BATH

Lorenz books is an imprint of
Anness Publishing Inc.
27 West 20th Street
New York, NY 10011

© Anness Publishing Limited 1997

ISBN 1 85967 511 5

*Publisher:* Joanna Lorenz
*Senior Editor:* Clare Nicholson
*Designer:* Michael Morey
*Photographer:* Peter Anderson

Printed in Hong Kong

3 5 7 9 10 8 6 4 2

# Contents

# Introduction

*F*rom the elegant species to the showiest large-flowered hybrids, there are clematis to suit every taste and style of garden. Some dazzle with their huge, luminescent flowers; others smother themselves with starry flowers that are often scented. Several are quiet plants that enchant with their dainty flowers, often peeping shyly through the foliage of a host plant. There is a clematis for every site, against a wall, into a tree, on a pergola, in the herbaceous border or – where space is limited – in a container. Such is the range available that by judicious selection it is possible to enjoy a clematis in flower virtually every month of the year. This book shows you how to grow all types of clematis and how to enjoy them to the full. It also illustrates some of the finest examples now available.

■ RIGHT
*C. montana* 'Elizabeth' cloaking a garden wall in early spring.

# The history of clematis

There are more than 230 species of clematis, found in both hemispheres (chiefly the northern), in Europe, the Himalaya, China, North and Central America, Africa and Australasia. In Europe, the native *C. vitalba* (old man's beard or traveller's joy) is a familiar sight, festooning hedgerows and woodland margins with its creamy-white flowers, followed by fluffy grey seedheads in autumn.

Exactly when clematis began to be cultivated in European gardens is not known, but there are references to *C. vitalba* in 16th-century English herbals. *C. viticella*, later to become important in clematis breeding, was being grown outside its native

The North American *C. viorna,* though itself a rarity in gardens, has been much used in hybridizing.

Mediterranean habitat during the reign of Elizabeth I. Other European species cultivated in gardens by the end of the 16th century were *C. cirrhosa,* and the herbaceous *C. recta* and *C. integrifolia.* A cross between *C. viticella* and *C. integrifolia* resulted in *C. x eriostemon.* Later came *C. alpina* and, from further afield, *C. flammula* and *C. tangutica.* All remain highly valued garden plants that are still widely grown.

In 1776 *C. florida* was introduced from Japan (the species also occurs in China). Other significant introductions were two large-flowered species from China, *C. patens* (1840, which is also found in Japan) and *C. lanuginosa* (1850). These three species opened up hitherto unimagined breeding possibilities and led to the development of the large-flowered hybrids we enjoy today. *C. florida* has a double-flowered

■ LEFT
*C. texensis*, from the USA, is the parent of many late-flowering hybrids that have inherited its tulip-like flowers.

■ BELOW
'Burford Variety', which is a hybrid between *C. tibetana* ssp. *vernayi* and *C. tangutica.*

bred in Belgium and Switzerland. A few unsurpassed cultivars from that era still survive, including 'Nelly Moser' and 'The President', as well as the ubiquitous 'Jackmanii'. In the first part of the 20th century the number of cultivars decreased, possibly because excessive hybridization had resulted in weaker plants. There was a resurgence of interest in the genus after World War II, however, and today there are at least 600 cultivars in commerce, with newcomers being added all the time.

cultivar, 'Flore Pleno', and it was possibly genes from this plant that produced some of the sumptuous double hybrids.

One of the first, and best, of the new large-flowered hybrids was 'Jackmanii' (raised in Surrey, Great Britain). This has given its name to a whole group of cultivars, the Jackmanii Group. Other important introductions were the American *C. texensis* and *C. viorna*, both with pendent, urn-shaped flowers.

By the end of the 19th century there were well over 300 large-flowered clematis cultivars in commerce, not all of good quality; most were raised in Britain, France and Germany, though some were

■ BELOW
The early-flowering *C. cirrhosa*, a European species, produces delicate, nodding flowers. This heavily spotted form is named 'Freckles'.

# Clematis in the garden

## Seasonal interest

Clematis are among the most versatile of garden plants. There is a clematis for virtually every garden situation and, by carefully choosing among the species and cultivars, it is possible to have a clematis in flower almost every month of the year. Some are quiet plants in subdued shades of mauve or delicate blue, while others are more showy attention-seekers, rightly deserving prime positions in the garden.

The earliest to flower in most gardens is the winter-flowering *C. cirrhosa*, a delicate-looking, though usually hardy, evergreen clematis from the Mediterranean with bell-like, creamy-green flowers; var. *balearica* has flowers spotted with maroon-red on the inside. In cold spells the foliage tinges bronze, an added attraction. In early spring the *C. macropetala* and *C. alpina* cultivars begin their display, with elegant, nodding blooms in shades of blue, pink, mauve and white.

Two rampant species follow. *C. montana*, with masses of star-shaped flowers, can make an enormous plant that covers 6m (20ft) or more in either direction, and is breathtaking in full flower. It has

several desirable cultivars, some less
rampant, including the scented, soft
pink 'Elizabeth' or the orange-tinted
'Marjorie', the latter with more
elegant flowers. The other monster is
*C. armandii*, an evergreen with
distinctive, long, almost leathery
leaves and deliciously scented flowers.
In cold climates it prefers a warm wall.

As spring turns to summer the
large-flowered hybrids, most in
shades of white, mauve or pink, begin
to make their presence felt. They are
high-value clematis that often put on
a repeat performance in mid- to late
summer. Among the showiest are
those with double flowers, such as
'Beauty of Worcester' (deep blue),
'Proteus' (mauve pink) and 'Vyvyan
Pennell' (rich lilac).

At the peak of the season you are
spoilt for choice among the hybrids.
Some of the best loved are 'Perle
d'Azur', with azure-blue flowers,
'Purpurea Plena Elegans', with small,
double, dusky pink flowers and
'Duchess of Edinburgh', with double
white flowers tinged with green. Later,
as the Texensis and Viticella types
begin to make their mark, the
predominant colours change to rich
wine reds, purples and violets. Most
cultivars deriving from *C. texensis* have
small, elegant, tulip-shaped flowers.

The Viticella types mostly have small,
open flowers.

The several herbaceous clematis
also flower in summer and they are
excellent garden plants. Among them
are *C. recta*, with star-shaped, white
flowers, and *C. heracleifolia*, with
narrow, bell-shaped, blue flowers;
both are highly fragrant.

Then there are several late-
flowering species. *C. tibetana* ssp.
*vernayi* and *C. tangutica* (sometimes

classed as *C. orientalis* in horticulture)
are similar, with bell-shaped yellow
flowers, that are followed by attractive fluffy seedheads. *C. flammula* and
*C. rehderiana* are two heavily scented,
rampant species that take the clematis
season into autumn. Less vigorous
and certainly less widely grown are
*C. potaninii* var. *fargesii*, with saucer-
shaped white flowers, and *C.
terniflora*, similar to *C. flammula* but
without its potent fragrance.

## Plant arrangements and associations

Clematis can be grown in a variety of ways, on pergolas, against walls and fences, and the more vigorous into trees; a few are suitable for growing in containers. Vigorous *C. montana* types are ideal for clothing ugly buildings and sheds, though the coverage is not evergreen. These and other large species, such as *C. flammula* and *C. rehderiana*, can also be grown into trees, provided the trees are strong enough to bear the weight of the clematis.

Many of the hybrids are best grown against walls, the more vigorous also being good candidates for arbours and pergolas. They can also be planted in the border to scramble up pillars or tripods. For a more unusual way of growing clematis, make a flowering table by supporting a horizontal trellis panel flat on low uprights in the border, and training the plant over it. Since the flowers will appear at a lower level than usual, you do not have to crane your neck to appreciate their beauty.

The most valued use of clematis, however, is in conjunction with other plants. Clematis can be planted to grow into shrubs to provide a show of

■ ABOVE
**Grouping several large-flowered hybrids that bloom simultaneously ensures a sumptuous display.**

■ LEFT
**'Purpurea Plena Elegans' provides the interest now that its host plant, *Rosa* 'Climbing Cécile Brünner', has all but finished flowering.**

■ OPPOSITE
**In a mixed border, large-flowered 'Lasurstern' and the herbaceous *C. recta* 'Purpurea' vie for attention with *Euonymus* 'Silver Queen' in the foreground.**

interest either before or after the host plant has flowered, or to coincide with it. The less vigorous, late-flowering clematis that will not swamp other plants are best for this purpose, since you can prune them when you tidy up the borders in early spring (see Pruning and training). Good choices would be 'Beauty of Richmond' (greyish-lavender), 'Mme Grangé' (velvety purple) or 'Etoile Violette' (rich violet-purple). The Texensis types – such as 'Etoile Rose' (deep rose-pink) and 'Gravetye Beauty' (rich crimson-red) – have a rustic character. The Viticella types are like smaller versions of large-flowered types and include 'Mme Julia Correvon' (wine-red) and 'Royal Velours' (rich crimson), or *C. viticella* itself (bright purple). You can also plant clematis to clamber up a more formally trained plant, such as a climbing rose. It does not matter if the clematis is not smothered with flowers; simply allow the clematis flowers to peep through the host plant here and there. For a cool, striking combination try 'Ascotiensis' (violet-blue) with the old-fashioned

■ LEFT
'Bees' Jubilee' rambling over a
rhododendron in light woodland.

contrast against a purple-leaved shrub
such as a *Berberis* or *Cotinus*, but will
look more subtle as the silvery-grey
seedheads that succeed the flowers
begin to dominate.

For a sophisticated look, try
combining 'Ville de Lyon' (carmine-
red) or 'Purpurea Plena Elegans'
(dusky pink) with the ornamental
vine, *Vitis vinifera* 'Purpurea' (plum-
purple), or the violet-pink rose, *Rosa*
'Veilchenblau'. In a white garden,
choose from the passion flower-like,
slightly tender, *C. florida* 'Sieboldii',
with striking contrasting purple
staminodes, 'Gillian Blades', 'Henryi',
'Huldine', 'Jackmanii Alba', 'John
Huxtable' or 'Marie Boisselot'.

rambler rose 'Albéric Barbier'
(creamy-white). In a wild garden you
could create a wonderful autumn
show by growing *C. rehderiana* and a
Virginia creeper (*Parthenocissus
quinquefolia*) into a mature apple or
pear tree, provided it can take the
strain. The individual clematis
flowers are not particularly
spectacular, but they are abundant,
and their creamy-yellow colouring

would look entrancing mingled with
the reddening foliage of the creeper.

Alternatively, go for a deep
contrast by planting the rich purple
'Jackmanii Superba' or the maroon
'Rouge Cardinal' into the golden-
leaved hop (*Humulus lupulus*
'Aureus'). Any of the three, roughly
similar, yellow clematis, *C. tibetana*
ssp. *vernayi*, *C. tangutica* or 'Bill
MacKenzie', will provide a strong

■ ABOVE

The Orientalis group have lovely yellow flowers from mid-summer to autumn, and then they have an extravagant display of fruits. This group is widely cultivated in gardens today, and includes plants such as 'Bill MacKenzie' and *C. tangutica*.

■ OPPOSITE

'The President', one of the first large-flowered hybrids to bloom, loosely trained to a stake in a border.

In a border herbaceous clematis are unassuming plants, and blend easily with other perennials, such as anthemis, rudbeckias, phloxes, geraniums and penstemons. Their scent is a bonus. They tend to be weak-growing, however, so either stake them or allow them to flop over graciously into other plants.

On a patio, balcony, terrace, or roof garden, there are many clematis that are well suited to growing in containers and which can be trained up small trellises. All of the *C. macropetala* cultivars and many of the smaller-growing hybrids, such as 'Carnaby' (deep pink) or 'Snow Queen' (white), can be grown in this way by town gardeners who, even if they do not have much space, will quickly appreciate the clematis's extraordinary beauty and charm.

# The clematis plant

Members of the buttercup family (Ranunculaceae), clematis are mainly woody or semi-woody climbers; the genus also includes some woody-based herbaceous perennials. Clematis are generally hardy plants and most are deciduous. Evergreen clematis are usually less hardy and, in cold climates, benefit from being grown against a warm sheltered wall (see also Cultivation). There are a number of sub-tropical species that cannot survive temperatures below 0°C (32°F), and which must be grown under glass in cold climates. The climbers mostly attach

themselves by means of leaf stalks that twist around their support (usually the stems of a host plant in the wild). Herbaceous types have lax stems.

The majority of the species have small flowers, borne either singly or in clusters or panicles. Clematis flowers are unusual in having no true petals. In most other genera the flowers are enclosed within green sepals that split open to reveal coloured petals. In the case of the clematis petals are absent, but the sepals are coloured like petals. The sepals usually number from 4 to 10; some flowers have many more.

At the centre of each flower are the reproductive parts, consisting of a large boss of stamens (which carry the pollen) surrounding the female part of the flower (later this develops into the seedheads). The anthers or stamens are prominent; in some cases they are a decorative, distin-guishing feature. In the species *C. macropetala* some of the outer stamens are petal-like, giving the flower a double or semi-double appearance. In the case of the double, large-flowered hybrid clematis, the anthers are modified into petal-like structures.

The open star-like
flowers of *C. montana.*

A Viticella-type clematis.

A yellow-flowered
hybrid clematis.

Flower colours range from white through all shades of pink to red, blue and purple; but often the blues tend towards mauve and the reds towards blue, turning them magenta, wine-red or maroon rather than clear red. Yellow occurs in the species *C. tibetana* and *C. tangutica* and their hybrids but has not been bred into any of the large-flowered types.

In the case of some large-flowered hybrids, flower size and colour may vary across the season, later flowers tending to be smaller and more intense in colour. Once open, most hybrid clematis flowers become paler, especially in strong sunlight, and several shades may be present on the plant at any one time.

Hybrid clematis are divided into the following groups: Florida Group, Jackmanii Group, Lanuginosa Group, Patens Group, Texensis Group and Viticella Group. The flower forms found in the first four are broadly similar (though the Jackmanii Group includes no doubles), so only the Viticella and Texensis types are commonly referred to. Both of these have unmistakable flowers. However, gardeners usually divide all clematis into three broad groups according to their flowering season. This division is also useful in determining pruning needs (for further details see Pruning and training).

*Group 1* The clematis have flowers borne on the previous year's growth in late winter to spring.

*Group 2* The clematis have flowers in two flushes, the first in late spring to early summer on the previous year's wood, the second in mid- to late summer on new wood.

*Group 3* The clematis flower on the current season's growth from mid-summer to late autumn.

The feathery
seedhead of
*C. tangutica.*

The bell-shaped flowers of
*C. macropetala.*

A large-flowered hybrid
clematis and seedhead.

# Plant Catalogue

# Group 1

In this gallery, clematis are divided according to their flowering season as follows.

***Group 1*** Climbing species and their cultivars that flower from late winter to spring.

***Group 2*** Hybrids that flower in late spring and early summer, and again from mid- to late summer. The flowers are 10–20cm (4–8in) across; in some cases, the early flowers are double.

***Group 3*** Clematis that flower from mid-summer to autumn. The group includes: large-flowered hybrids, with flowers 7.5–15cm (3–6in) across; texensis types, with tulip-like flowers to 5cm (2in) long; viticella types, with flowers to 7.5cm (3in) across; some species, all with small flowers; and herbaceous types.

The heights and spreads cited are those the plants can be expected to achieve given good cultivation in five years, but they are approximate. Size will vary according to the local climate, soil type and season. Flowering times may also vary from year to year, and will also depend on the season.

■ LEFT

### C. MONTANA 'CONTINUITY'

Cultivar of *C. montana* from western and central China, and the Himalaya. From late spring to early summer it produces an abundance of star-like, creamy-white, pink-tinged flowers to 5cm (2in) across. Height and spread to 6m (20ft) or more. *C. montana* 'Continuity' is shown here growing through a mature golden conifer. It has the longest flowering season of all the *montana* cultivars – hence the name.

■ BELOW

### 'ROSY O'GRADY'

Hybrid clematis, often listed under *C. macropetala* but with more of the characteristics of *C. alpina*. From spring to early summer, it carries nodding bell-shaped, semi-double, bright pinkish-mauve flowers, 7cm (2¾in) across, that are succeeded by fluffy, silvery seedheads. Height to 3m (10ft), spread 1.5m (5ft). 'Rosy O'Grady' sometimes produces a few further flowers in autumn.

■ OPPOSITE ABOVE

### C. ARMANDII 'SNOWDRIFT'

Cultivar of *C. armandii* from China. In spring, it carries clusters of saucer-shaped, fragrant, waxy white flowers, to 6.5cm (2½in) across, among evergreen, lance-shaped, leathery, dark green leaves. Height and spread to 9m (30ft). In cold climates *C. armandii* 'Snowdrift' is best grown against a warm wall.

■ OPPOSITE BELOW

### C. CIRRHOSA (SYN. C. CALYCINA)

Evergreen species clematis from Europe. In late winter and early spring, it produces delicate, nodding, cup-shaped, pink-tinged, creamy-white flowers, 6cm (2¼in) long, that are sometimes speckled with brownish-red inside. Height 3m (10ft), spread 1.5m (5ft). The fern-like foliage of *C. cirrhosa* often tinges bronze during cold weather, an added attraction.

# Group 2

■ ABOVE
### 'BEES' JUBILEE'

Large-flowered clematis. In spring it produces masses of single, deep mauve-pink flowers, 13cm (5⅛in) across, that lighten with age, each sepal having a darker central bar; the anthers are light brown. A second flush of smaller flowers appears in mid- to late summer. Height 2.4m (8ft), spread 90cm (3ft). 'Bees' Jubilee', a compact and reliable clematis, is best in partial shade because it fades badly in strong sunlight; it is similar to the more commonly grown 'Nelly Moser'.

■ ABOVE
### 'BARBARA DIBLEY'

Large-flowered clematis. In spring it carries single, bright cerise-pink flowers, 15cm (6in) across, with the sepals marked with a central darker bar; further flowers are produced in mid- to late summer. Height 2.4m (8ft), spread 90cm (3ft). 'Barbara Dibley' tolerates any aspect but full shade.

■ OPPOSITE BELOW
### 'FIREWORKS'

Large-flowered clematis. From early to late summer it produces masses of single, luminous violet flowers, each sepal barred with mauve-carmine; the anthers are white tipped with carmine. Height 4m (13ft), spread 90cm (3ft). 'Fireworks', a striking, aptly named clematis, tolerates any aspect.

■ RIGHT

'DUCHESS OF EDINBURGH'

Large-flowered clematis. In late spring to early summer it produces
dahlia-like, double white flowers, 10cm (4in) across, tinged with
green, and with pale yellow anthers; there is a further flush of
blooms in late summer. Height 3m (10ft), spread 90cm (3ft).
'Duchess of Edinburgh' benefits from good cultivation since it can
be a weak grower. Apply a foliar feed during the growing season.

■ BELOW

*C. FLORIDA* 'ALBA PLENA'

Cultivar of *C. florida* from China and Japan. In late spring to early summer, and again in mid- to late summer, it carries double, passion flower-like, greenish-white flowers, 8cm (3¼in) across. Height 2m (6½ft), spread 90cm (3ft). A choice plant, *C. florida* 'Alba Plena', here supported by a ceanothus, is weak-growing and benefits from good cultivation; less hardy than some other popular clematis, in cooler climates it needs a warm, sheltered position. Propagation can be difficult.

■ ABOVE

'GILLIAN BLADES'

Large-flowered clematis. In late spring to early summer, and again from mid-summer, it bears large, single white flowers with cream anthers; the sepals overlap slightly and have wavy margins. Height 2.4m (8ft), spread 90cm (3ft). 'Gillian Blades' tolerates any aspect.

■ RIGHT

**'LASURSTERN'**

Large-flowered clematis. In early summer,
and again from mid-summer, it produces
masses of flowers, 13cm (5¼in) across, that
have wavy-edged sepals and are mauve-
blue, fading to silvery-mauve; the anthers
are cream. Height 2.4m (8ft), spread 90cm
(3ft). 'Lasurstern' tolerates any aspect
except full shade.

■ LEFT

**'JOHN WARREN'**

Large-flowered clematis. In late spring to
early summer, and again from mid-
summer, it produces single flowers, 13cm
(5¼in) across, that have long, pointed,
overlapping, pale greyish-pink sepals,
veined and edged deeper pink, and red
anthers. Height 3m (10ft), spread 90cm
(3ft). A compact variety of unique colour,
'John Warren' is shown here matched
with the grey-leaved Jerusalem sage
(*Phlomis fruticosa*).

■ ABOVE
'MRS GEORGE JACKMAN'

Large-flowered clematis. In late spring it produces semi-double,
creamy-white flowers, 10cm (4in) across, with pale brown anthers;
later flowers (from mid- to late summer) are single. Height 2.4m
(8ft), spread 90cm (3ft). 'Mrs George Jackman' tolerates any aspect
but full shade.

■ ABOVE
'MRS CHOLMONDELEY'

Large-flowered clematis. From late spring to late summer it has single, pale lavender-blue flowers, to 13cm (5¼in) across, with non-overlapping sepals; the anthers are chocolate-brown. Height 3m (10ft), spread 90cm (3ft). 'Mrs Cholmondeley' has one of the longest flowering seasons of all clematis; early flowers sometimes open green, particularly in cold weather.

■ ABOVE LEFT
'MARIE BOISSELOT'

Large-flowered clematis. From summer to late autumn it carries striking, single white flowers, 13cm (5¼in) across, with sepals that overlap; the anthers are cream. Height 3m (10ft), spread 90cm (3ft). Justifiably one of the most popular of the white-flowered clematis, 'Marie Boisselot' is sometimes sold as 'Mme le Coultre'; almost uniquely among clematis, it holds its flowers horizontally.

■ ABOVE RIGHT
'NELLY MOSER'

Large-flowered clematis. In early and late summer it has single, wavy-edged, pinkish-mauve flowers, 12.5–15cm (5–6in) across, barred with carmine pink; the anthers are rust red. Height 3m (10ft), spread 90cm (3ft). An old variety, 'Nelly Moser' is justifiably one of the most popular of all clematis.

■ RIGHT
'SILVER MOON'

Large-flowered clematis. From late spring
to early summer and again from mid-
summer to autumn, it produces large,
gleaming, lavender-white flowers with
cream anthers. Height 1.8m (6ft), spread
90cm (3ft). 'Silver Moon' needs careful
placing in the garden, owing to its subtle
colouring. Here *Cotoneaster integrifolius* is
the perfect foil.

■ LEFT
'ROYALTY'

Large-flowered clematis. In late spring to summer it produces an
abundance of semi-double, purplish-mauve flowers, 15cm (6in)
across, with pale yellow anthers; later flowers, from mid-summer to
autumn, are smaller and single. Height 1.8m (6ft), spread 90cm
(3ft). 'Royalty' tolerates any aspect.

# Group 3

### 'ALLANAH'

Large-flowered clematis. From mid- to late summer it produces single, bright ruby-red flowers, 15cm (6in) across, with non-overlapping sepals; the anthers are chocolate-brown. Height 2.4m (8ft), spread 90cm (3ft). 'Allanah' is shown here wandering through a planting of the blue grass, *Leymus arenarius.*

### 'BILL MACKENZIE'

Clematis similar to *C. tibetana* and *C. tangutica*, probably a hybrid between the two. From mid-summer to autumn it carries masses of thick-sepalled, bright yellow, lantern-like flowers, 5cm (2in) across when fully open; the anthers are red. Attractive, fluffy, silver-grey seedheads follow. Height 7m (23ft), spread to 3m (10ft). 'Bill MacKenzie' has larger flowers than either of the species from which it is said to derive.

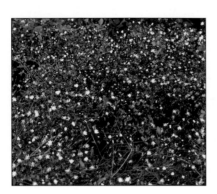

■ RIGHT AND ABOVE

*C. x AROMATICA*

Sprawling or semi-erect, non-climbing
hybrid clematis, a cross between
*C. flammula* and *C. integrifolia*. From
summer to autumn, it produces masses of
heavily scented, deep violet flowers, 4cm
(1½in) across. Height and spread to 2m
(6½ft). An unusual clematis, *C. x
aromatica* can be allowed to flop over into
neighbouring plants or can be trained
against a wall.

■ RIGHT

'DUCHESS OF ALBANY'

Texensis-type clematis. From mid-summer
to early autumn it bears small, tulip-
shaped, warm pink flowers, 6cm (2½in)
long, banded with red; the anthers are
brown. Height 2.4m (8ft), spread 1.5m
(5ft). 'Duchess of Albany' is a fairly
vigorous clematis that tolerates any aspect
but full shade.

■ ABOVE
### C. FLAMMULA

Species clematis from southern Europe, north Africa, and western Asia. In late summer and early autumn it produces masses of star-shaped, cowslip-scented, creamy-white flowers, 2cm (¾in) across; silver-grey seedheads follow. Height 6m (20ft), spread 3m (10ft). Good for growing through a tree, *C. flammula* does best in a sheltered, sunny site and tolerates poor soil.

■ ABOVE RIGHT
### C. HERACLEIFOLIA 'WYEVALE'

Herbaceous clematis, a cultivar of a species from China. In late summer it produces clusters of very fragrant, rich blue flowers, 2.5cm (1in) long, on thick stems. Height and spread 90cm (3ft). Attractive to bees and butterflies, *C. heracleifolia* 'Wyevale' is a valuable addition to the border; it benefits from staking.

■ RIGHT
### 'GRAVETYE BEAUTY'

Texensis-type clematis. In mid-summer to autumn it bears tulip-like, red flowers, 6cm (2½in) long, with pink reverses to the sepals; the flowers open further, eventually to a star shape. Height 2.4m (8ft), spread 90cm (3ft). The flowers of 'Gravetye Beauty' are the clearest red of any clematis cultivar.

■ ABOVE
'HULDINE'

Large-flowered clematis. From mid- to
late summer it produces single, pearly-
white flowers, 5cm (2in) across, with
sepals that curve back and are mauve
beneath; the anthers are cream. Height
3m (10ft), spread 2m (6½ft). 'Huldine' is
one of the daintiest of all the Group 3
climbers, but flowering is not reliably free;
the flowers are similar to those of 'John
Huxtable' but smaller.

■ RIGHT
'JACKMANII SUPERBA'

Large-flowered clematis. From mid-
to late summer it produces an
abundance of velvety, rich purple
flowers, 15cm (6in) across, with
light brown anthers. Height 3m
(10ft), spread 90cm (3ft). 'Jackmanii
Superba' is similar in colour and
habit to the popular 'Jackmanii' but
has darker flowers, with slightly
wider sepals.

■ ABOVE AND RIGHT

## C. x *JOUINIANA* 'PRAECOX'

Sprawling, non-climbing clematis with scandent stems (long and flexible, but
with no means of attaching themselves
to a support). It is a hybrid between
*C. heracleifolia* var. *davidiana* and
*C. vitalba.* In late summer it produces
hyacinth-like, pale purplish-blue flowers,
2cm (⅜in) across, that are overlaid with
silver. Height 90cm (3ft), spread 3m (10ft).
*C.* x *jouiniana* 'Praecox' is best planted as
ground cover, or among low-growing shrubs
that will support the lax stems; it can be fan-
trained against a wall.

■ RIGHT

'KERMESINA'

Viticella-type clematis. From late summer to autumn it carries masses of deep crimson flowers, 3–5cm (1¼–2in) across, with reddish-brown anthers. Height 4m (13ft), spread 2m (6½ft). 'Kermesina' tolerates any position but full shade.

■ LEFT

'PAGODA'

Texensis-type clematis. In mid-summer to autumn, it bears tulip-like, warm pinkish-red flowers, 6cm (2½in) long, with sharply upturned sepals. Height 2.5m (8ft), spread 1m (3ft). 'Pagoda' is aptly named in view of the unique shape of its flowers.

■ ABOVE

'PURPUREA PLENA ELEGANS'

Viticella-type clematis. From mid-summer
to early autumn it produces masses of fully
double, deep purplish-pink flowers, to
7.5cm (3in) across; the reverse of the sepals
is a contrasting pinkish grey. Height 3m
(10ft), spread 90cm (3ft). 'Purpurea Plena
Elegans', one of the most striking clematis
of its type, tolerates any aspect.

■ RIGHT

*C. RECTA* 'PURPUREA'

Herbaceous clematis, a cultivar of a species
from central and southern Europe. From
mid-summer to autumn it produces an
abundance of fragrant, creamy-white
flowers, to 2cm (¾in) across, on purplish-
green stems; the young foliage is also
flushed purple. Height 2.1m (7ft), spread
90cm (3ft). *C. recta* 'Purpurea', a more
striking plant than the species on account
of its coloured stems, needs staking.

■ LEFT AND BELOW
*C. REHDERIANA*

Species clematis from the Himalaya and western China. From late summer to autumn it carries an abundance of bell-shaped, fragrant, creamy-yellow flowers, 2cm (¾in) long. Height 6m (20ft), spread 3m (10ft). Magnificent when grown into a medium-sized tree or over a wall, *C. rehderiana* tolerates any aspect.

■ LEFT
'ROUGE CARDINAL'

Large-flowered clematis. From mid-summer to autumn it has dusky red flowers, 7.5–10cm (3–4in) across, with reddish-brown anthers. Height 3m (10ft), spread 90cm (3ft). 'Rouge Cardinal' succeeds best in full sun.

■ ABOVE
### 'ROYAL VELOURS'

Viticella-type clematis. From mid-summer
to autumn it produces velvety, deep
purplish-red flowers, to 7.5cm (3in) across.
Height to 6m (20ft), spread 3m (10ft).
Sometimes confused with 'Royal Velvet',
'Royal Velours' is the superior plant; its
flowers are the deepest colour of any of the
viticella hybrids.

■ RIGHT
### C. TANGUTICA

Species clematis from Mongolia, North-
west China and North Tibet (Xizang).
From mid-summer to autumn it produces
an abundance of small, nodding, pointed,
lantern-like flowers, 4cm (1½in) long, with
thick yellow sepals; decorative, fluffy
silvery-grey seedheads follow. Height 6m
(20ft), spread 3m (10ft). *C. tangutica* is
often confused in cultivation with the
similar *C. tibetana* and 'Bill MacKenzie',
which is possibly a hybrid between the
two species.

■ LEFT

### *C. x TRITERNATA* 'RUBROMARGINATA'

Hybrid clematis, a selection of a cross between *C. flammula* and *C. viticella*. From late summer to autumn it produces a profusion of small, pink, fragrant flowers, 2.5cm (1in) across, the sepals edged with deep purple-red. Height 3m (10ft), spread 90cm (3ft).
*C. x triternata* 'Rubromarginata', a plant of considerable distinction, is shown here rambling through a wisteria; it tolerates any aspect.

■ RIGHT

### 'VICTORIA'

Large-flowered clematis. From mid-summer to autumn it produces rose-purple flowers, 10cm (4in) across, that fade to mauve; the anthers are brown. Height 3m (10ft), spread 90cm (3ft). 'Victoria' is a good subject for growing through a medium-sized tree.

■ LEFT

'VILLE DE LYON'

Large-flowered clematis. From mid-summer to early autumn it bears deep pinkish-red flowers, 7.5–10cm (3–4in) across, with golden-yellow anthers. Height 3m (10ft), spread 90cm (3ft). 'Ville de Lyon', one of the most popular "red" clematis, appreciates a sunny site.

■ BELOW

'VIVIENNE LAWSON'

Large-flowered clematis. From mid-summer to early autumn, it carries rich purplish-blue flowers, to 10cm (4in) across, with golden-yellow anthers. Height 3m (10ft), spread 90cm (3ft). 'Vivienne Lawson' tolerates a shady site.

# Buying clematis

Clematis are sold in garden centres, and by mail order from specialist nurseries, as pot-grown plants in containers usually about 18cm (7in) across. When buying at a garden centre look for strong-growing plants that have plenty of shoots near the base. Reject any that show obvious signs of disease or damage, and those with lots of roots growing through the holes at the base of the pot, indicating that the plant is pot-bound.

Where practical at the point of sale, slide the plant from its pot and check that the root system is healthy.

If the roots are coiled tightly around the pot they will continue to grow in a spiral once the plant is in the ground, making it slow to establish.

Garden centres often like to sell plants that are in flower. While this means that you can be certain that the plant is the one you want, note that it will establish no more quickly than a non-flowering plant.

Smaller plants are sometimes available in supermarkets and grocery stores, usually at the beginning and end of the flowering season. Though cheaper, they take longer to establish,

Most clematis are sold in 18cm (7in) pots. Look for strong-growing plants with plenty of shoots arising from the base of the plant.

Small plants with fewer stems are sometimes available. They are usually cheap but need good aftercare to ensure they establish themselves properly.

Check the root system by sliding the clematis from its container. Reject the plant if the roots are congested or tightly coiled around the pot. The root system of this plant is in good condition.

■ BELOW
The choice species *C. potannii* var.
*potaninii*, from western China, is a
woodlander that thrives in shade.

and only the more popular varieties
are likely to be on offer. They are
often best if potted on and planted
out the following year.

Clematis are usually sold with
their stems tied to canes. Though
they are often tangled this is not a
drawback, since it is good practice to
shorten all stems the first spring after
flowering, to establish a strong-
growing plant (see Pruning and
training). The canes should be

**CLEMATIS SUITABLE
FOR GROWING IN
SHADE**

*C. alpina* and cultivars

'Bees' Jubilee'

'Comtesse de Bouchaud'

'Duchess of Edinburgh'

'Hagley Hybrid'

'Henryi'

'Jackmanii'

'John Huxtable'

*C. macropetala* and cultivars

'Miss Bateman'

'Mrs Cholmondeley'

'Nelly Moser'

'Perle d'Azur'

'Ramona'

'The President'

'Wada's Primrose'

'William Kennett'

removed on planting and, as far as
possible, the stems unravelled, but
care should be taken not to damage
the brittle young growth.

Container-grown clematis can be
planted at any time of the year except
when the ground is frozen or waterlogged, or during periods of prolonged drought.

**CLEMATIS SUITABLE FOR
GROWING IN FULL SUN**

*C. armandii*

*C. cirrhosa* and forms

*C. florida* and cultivars

*C. tangutica*

*C. tibetana*

# Cultivation

Clematis will grow in most soils, though they dislike very acid and poorly drained soils. The ideal soil is a fertile, moist but well-drained loam. For the best results increase soil fertility by digging in organic matter, such as garden compost, well-rotted farmyard manure or spent mushroom compost. The last is particularly recommended since it tends to be alkaline. Additions of organic matter also improve soil texture. They open up heavy clay soils that are slow to warm up in spring and help light, free-draining soils, that dry out easily, retain moisture and nutrients. If you have very heavy soil, you can add grit as well as garden compost to improve the drainage.

Established plants benefit from an annual mulch of organic matter in spring. A handful of bonemeal forked in around the base of the plant in late winter or early spring promotes good root growth. Additional feeding is not usually needed, but where the soil is poor quality or the clematis are in competition with other plants for nutrients, fork in a general fertilizer, a proprietary rose fertilizer or pelleted chicken manure in spring.

Water newly planted clematis regularly during the first growing season to ensure they establish well. In subsequent years watering should not be necessary, except where the soil is excessively dry (at the base of a wall, for instance) or during periods of prolonged drought in summer. Bear in mind, however, that a hot, dry spell can be beneficial to plants, stimulating the roots to grow downwards in search of the moisture available at lower levels, causing top-growth to cease and the stems to ripen. The net result is a healthier, sturdier plant. If you need to water, irrigate the plants in the evening to prevent excessive evaporation from the soil surface. A copious drink ensures that the water penetrates as deep as possible.

Clematis enjoy a cool root run and like to be planted with their roots in the shade and their top-growth in the sun. Clematis vary in their tolerance of full sun – most are best with some

Good, fertile loam is crumbly in texture, well-drained and includes decayed vegetable matter.

In late winter or early spring, fork in a handful of bonemeal around the base of an established plant.

Clematis benefit from an annual mulch of humus-rich organic matter (in this case spent mushroom compost) in spring.

Wrapping chicken wire around the trunk of this tree has provided support for a clematis. In a fairly open situation, as here, keep the roots cool by placing tiles or pavers over them.

A hardy fuchsia has been planted here to shade the roots of 'Bill MacKenzie'.

shade, particularly from hot summer sun. These conditions are easily achieved in the border by growing the clematis among shrubs that will shade their roots, but ensure that the clematis are never deprived of adequate moisture.

If planting against a wall, particularly if it is in the sun for much of the day, shade the roots in some way, either with a hard substance such as paving or slates, or by another plant. The former is likely to be more successful, since you can keep the roots cool without robbing them of moisture. On the other hand, clematis tend to become bare at the base, so planting them among shrubs and large herbaceous plants (especially against walls and fences) will help cover the unsightly lower half. Always choose your site with care, because clematis do not transplant easily: the roots of established plants are easily damaged and may never recover if disturbed.

Clematis wilt (see Pests and diseases) is the major problem with many large-flowered cultivars, seen as die-back in part or the whole of the plant. The causes of clematis wilt, which are not properly understood, can to some extent be alleviated by deep planting. Burying at least 10cm (4in) of the stem on planting encourages stem rooting, thus producing a plant with a stronger root system that is better able to recover from an attack of wilt. This also increases the number of shoots that are produced from the base each year.

# Planting clematis against a wall

Since clematis have no means of attaching themselves to a wall, you need to fix a trellis or a system of wires to the wall, against which you tie in the main stems as they grow. To ensure adequate air circulation between the plant and the wall, mount the trellis on battens. This also makes it easier to remove the plant from the wall if you need to paint or repair it.

Do note, however, that walls cast a rain shadow: the soil at the foot of the wall does not become as wet as that in the open border when it rains. Therefore, plant the clematis some distance away from the wall to ensure that the roots receive adequate moisture. During the first season you should water the plant regularly to ensure that it becomes properly established. Good soil preparation prior to planting is also essential if the clematis is to perform well, and will considerably reduce maintenance later on, since the plant will need less frequent watering and feeding.

PLANTING AGAINST A WALL

**1** (*right*) Select the position for the trellis and drill holes for the battens. Tap plastic plugs into the wall to take the screws.

**2** Cut battens to the appropriate size and screw them to the wall.

**3** Fix the trellis to the battens using rust-proof nails.

**4** Fork over the planting area, removing any perennial weeds and working in organic matter, such as garden compost or farmyard manure.

**5** Dig a hole at least 30cm (1ft) from the wall, and twice the width and depth of the plant's container, or deeper. Fork in more organic matter and a handful of bonemeal at the base.

**6** Place the clematis in the hole, and check the planting depth. Bury at least 10cm (4in) of stem.

**7** Water the plant well, then remove it from its pot and tease out the roots very carefully with a hand fork.

**8** Fan the roots away from the wall and angle the top-growth towards the support. Backfill with soil and firm in.

**9** Remove canes and spread the stems out. Tie them loosely to the support, just below a node (leaf joint), with wire ties twisted into a figure of eight or use horticultural twine.

**10** Water the plant and mulch with organic matter. To encourage stem rooting, place stones over the lower stems, between the nodes, to force them into contact with the soil.

The exotic-looking *C. florida* 'Sieboldii', not always reliably hardy, benefits from the protection of a south or south-west facing wall.

# Herbaceous clematis

Herbaceous clematis are sold as pot-grown plants in the same way as climbers. Prepare the site prior to planting, by digging over the soil, removing perennial weeds and forking in organic matter. After planting, water, mulch and feed as for a climbing clematis.

Herbaceous clematis are mostly weak-growing plants. You can set them among other perennials or dwarf shrubs that will support the clematis's floppy stems or insert a system of stakes on planting. Use either a ring stake or make a wigwam of hazel twigs to which you tie the stems as they grow. Check on the position of the stake when you cut back the dead growth early in the season (see Pruning and training).

You may need to substitute a larger ring stake as the plant matures; hazel twigs have to be replaced annually.

In time, herbaceous clematis grow to make large clumps. Forms of *C. heracleifolia* can run underground to some extent. Most herbaceous clematis are excellent for attracting insects into the garden, especially bees and butterflies.

■ RIGHT
A desirable
selection,
*C. integrifolia*
'Rosea' has sugar-pink flowers.

## PLANTING A HERBACEOUS CLEMATIS

1 Prepare the soil by removing any perennial weeds and working in organic matter. Dig a hole roughly twice the width and depth of the plant's container. Fork in bonemeal at the base of the hole to promote good root growth.

2 Water the plant thoroughly, then slide it out of its pot. To accelerate establishment, tease out some of the roots carefully with a handfork.

3 Check the planting depth. The crown of the plant should be level with the surrounding soil. Fill the hole around the roots. Firm in the plant.

4 Water the plant well, then position the ring stake, taking care that the uprights do not damage the crown. Set the ring stake fairly low to begin with. As the stems grow through the mesh, gradually raise the stake to support them. The top-growth will eventually hide the stake.

A combination that is both subtle and labour-saving: the stiff stems of *Sedum* 'Herbstfreude' (syn. 'Autumn Joy') support the fragrant *C. heracleifolia* var. *davidiana*.

# Growing clematis in containers

Among the numerous clematis cultivars available today, many are suitable for growing in containers. Choose from the smaller-growing species and hybrids. Given the restricted root run, clematis grown in pots will probably make smaller plants than those grown in the open garden but, with good feeding, will still have plenty of flowers.

### CLEMATIS FOR GROWING IN CONTAINERS

*C. alpina* and cultivars

'Asao'

'Carnaby'

'Comtesse de Bouchaud'

'Corona'

'Elsa Späth'

'Hagley Hybrid'

'H.F. Young'

'John Huxtable'

'John Warren'

'Kardynal Wyszynski'

*C. macropetala* and cultivars

'Mme Edouard André'

'Mme Julia Correvon'

'Miss Bateman'

'Niobe'

'Rouge Cardinal'

'Snow Queen'

'The President'

Growing clematis in containers brings several advantages. You can move the plant around the garden or patio at will, giving it a prominent position when in full flower, placing it in the background at other times. Take care, however, to avoid positions in full sun. The ideal location for a clematis in a container is one where the pots are shaded during the hot hours of the day. If placed in full sun, the top-growth will scorch and the roots dry out and overheat, particularly on a hard surface that reflects light and heat and which will bake the plant.

Ideally, choose a heavy container, either frost-proof terracotta or a wooden half-barrel. Since both are air and water permeable, the plant is less likely to become waterlogged than in a plastic container. However, if you have only a balcony or roof garden, where weight is a serious consideration, plastic may be your only option. Remember that the plant may need to be anchored in some way, since it will be top-heavy and might blow over in strong winds.

The clematis can be trained in exactly the same way as if it were growing in the open, so either insert

### PLANTING A CLEMATIS IN A CONTAINER

**1** Cover the base of the container with stones or crocks both for drainage and to provide added weight. Begin to fill the container with compost (soil mix).

**2** Check the planting depth. You should cover 10–15cm (4–6in) of the stem, allowing a gap of 2.5cm (1in) from the rim of the container for watering.

■ RIGHT
A clematis in a tall container with other container-grown plants of a similar colour range.

canes in the container, as shown here, or use a ready-made support. You can also train a container-grown clematis to a trellis panel fixed to a wall (see Planting clematis against a wall). An attractive alternative, however, is to dispense with training altogether and allow the plant to trail down the side of the container.

Clematis need fertile soil, so use a high-nutrient potting compost (potting soil). Regular watering is essential when the clematis is in full growth; this may have to be as often as once or twice a day during summer. For the best flowering, apply a high-potash fertilizer such as tomato feed.

**3** Remove the plant from its container and gently tease out some of the roots with a hand fork. This helps the plant to establish more quickly.

**4** Set the plant in the container and backfill. Water, then cover the surface with horticultural grit to stop water loss, and to keep the roots cool.

**5** Insert canes round the perimeter of the pot and link them together with wire or string to which you can tie the stems as they grow.

# Pruning and training

Most gardeners think the pruning of clematis is very complicated and confusing, but it is reasonably straightforward provided the pruning groups can be recognized.

Clematis are usually divided into three pruning groups, depending on their flowering season (see The clematis plant). Prune Group 1 clematis after flowering, and Groups 2 and 3 in late winter to early spring. Group 2 clematis can be pruned like Group 3 clematis to flower later in the season, but those cultivars that would normally have produced an initial crop of double flowers will probably bear single flowers only. After pruning, feed, water and mulch the plants well to promote recovery.

The instructions for tying in and training relate to clematis grown on trellis panels against walls, or on free-standing supports.

## Formative pruning

Formative pruning is beneficial to all clematis, encouraging the production of strong stems from near ground level. It prevents the clematis from becoming a top-heavy plant with only a few main stems and a mass of congested growth and flowers near the top.

The first spring after planting, unless the plant already has a number of strong stems emerging from the base, cut back all stems to about 30cm (1ft) from ground level. In the case of spring-flowering clematis (Group 1), the first season's flowers will be lost; on early summer-flowering types (Group 2), the first flush of flowers will be lost. This initial hard pruning, however, creates a stronger plant in the long run.

## Making the cuts

Since clematis buds lie opposite each other on the stem, cuts are made straight across. Always prune back to a strong, healthy pair of buds, cutting

When pruning, cut back to strong, healthy pairs of buds.

just above them. Use sharp secateurs. Rusty or blunt blades will snag the wood, providing an entry point for disease. When pruning an overgrown Group 1 clematis (see below), loppers or a pruning saw may be necessary to cut through thick, old stems.

## Tying in

Tie in shoots as close to the horizontal as possible. Place the tie just below a leaf joint and take care not to break the brittle stems. Horizontal training encourages the plant to flower over its entire surface. Stems allowed to grow upwards tend to flower only at their tips.

PRUNING GROUP 1

1 Shorten overlong shoots on Group 1 clematis in autumn, if necessary, though this may affect the flowering performance the following year.

Correctly pruned, 'Niobe' (Group 2) rewards the gardener with masses of warm red flowers throughout summer.

## Group 1

Group 1 clematis comprise species and their cultivars that flower before mid-summer, including both ever-green and deciduous types. After the initial pruning, tie in strong shoots as they develop. Thereafter, no regular pruning is necessary beyond removing dead, diseased or damaged growth. If the plant becomes congested, immediately after flowering cut back older stems to the base, then thin the top-growth, cutting back to a pair of healthy buds. You can also shorten over-long shoots in autumn, though this will limit the flowering next spring.

## Group 2

Group 2 clematis produce two flushes of flowers, the first on growth made the previous year, the second on new growth. Many of the large-flowered clematis fall into this category (the Florida, Lanuginosa and Patens Groups; see The clematis plant).

The first year after planting concentrate on building up a good framework by fanning out the stems. Thereafter, if the plant is performing well and fills its allotted space adequately, little or no pruning may be necessary. The following year, in late winter or early spring, just as the

new buds are beginning to burst, cut back to the ground any dead, diseased or damaged growth. You should also shorten or cut out completely any stems that cross or rub against each other. At the same time, shorten by up to a half any stems that have

PRUNING GROUP 2

**1** Towards the end of winter, a Group 2 clematis will probably present a tangled mass of stems.

**2** Prune some of the stems to healthy buds low down on the plant. These will produce strong new stems that will flower later in the season.

**3** Shorten any overlong stems, but leave some others unpruned, if possible. The first crop of flowers will be produced on this older wood.

outgrown their allotted space. The remaining stems will bear the first flowers on short laterals, but you should leave room for the new season's growth that will bear the second crop. Carefully tie in the new stems that appear after the first flowers.

To prolong the flowering season still further, cut back only a proportion of old stems initially. At regular intervals, cut back the remaining stems. This will stagger the onset of new growth, and flowering.

Group 2 clematis can also be pruned hard annually, like the Group 3 type. The first crop of flowers will be lost, but the later performance will be better. Double-flowered cultivars will normally produce single flowers only, however.

## Group 3

Group 3 clematis comprise species and hybrids that flower late in the season on the current year's growth, and herbaceous types. Group 3 clematis are pruned hard annually. With climbers, cut back all stems to a pair of healthy buds about 30cm (1ft) from the base. Any stems that do not bear buds at this level are probably dead and should be cut back to ground level. New replacement shoots will then arise from ground level.

Moderately vigorous clematis such as *C. tangutica*, *C. vitalba*, *C. aethusifolia*, *C. x jouiniana*, *C. rehderiana* and late large-flowered hybrids should be pruned in late winter for early flowering. Prune Texensis and Viticella types (that flower later) in early spring. The yellow-flowered *C. tangutica*, *C. tibetana* and *C.* 'Bill MacKenzie' can be pruned hard in late winter in a restricted area, or treated as Group 1 clematis and left largely unpruned if you want them to fill a large space. In this case, thin any congested growth in early spring, if necessary. Late large-flowered hybrids can also be pruned as for Group 2 clematis. This effectively extends the flowering season, since any stems that are left unpruned or are cut back only lightly, will flower earlier. The overall display may be less spectacular, however.

Cut herbaceous perennials back to strong shoots emerging from near ground level. Tie in new stems to the support with horticultural string as they grow.

### PRUNING GROUP 3

**1** At the end of winter, all the stems of Group 3 clematis will be bare. This is the time to prune all Group 3 clematis, except for Viticella and Texensis types which should be left until early spring.

**2** Cut back all stems to healthy buds within 30cm (1ft) of the base. Any stems that do not have strong growth buds can be cut back to the ground.

**3** With the onset of spring, a clematis pruned hard will rapidly make new growth.

## GROUP CHECK

The following is a checklist that indicates the pruning group of some of the most popular clematis described in this book ; * indicates varieties with double or semi-double flowers.

| SPECIES OR VARIETY | GROUP 1 | GROUP 2 | GROUP 3 |
|---|---|---|---|
| C. alpina and cultivars | ◆ | | |
| C. armandii and cultivars | ◆ | | |
| 'Barbara Dibley' | | ◆ | |
| 'Beauty of Worcester'* | | ◆ | |
| 'Bees' Jubilee' | | ◆ | |
| 'Belle of Woking'* | | ◆ | |
| 'Bill MacKenzie' | | | ◆ |
| 'Carnaby' | | ◆ | |
| C. cirrhosa and forms | ◆ | | |
| 'Comtesse de Bouchaud' | | | ◆ |
| 'Countess of Lovelace'* | | ◆ | |
| 'Duchess of Albany' | | | ◆ |
| 'Elsa Späth' | | ◆ | |
| x eriostemon and cultivars | | | ◆ |
| 'Etoile Rose' | | | ◆ |
| 'Etoile Violette' | | | ◆ |
| C. flammula | | | ◆ |
| C. florida and cultivars | | ◆ | |
| 'Gillian Blades' | | ◆ | |
| 'Gipsy Queen' | | | ◆ |
| 'Gravetye Beauty' | | | ◆ |
| 'Hagley Hybrid' | | | ◆ |
| 'Henryi' | | ◆ | |
| 'H.F. Young' | | ◆ | |
| 'Huldine' | | | ◆ |
| C. integrifolia and cultivars | | | ◆ |
| 'Jackmanii' | | | ◆ |

| SPECIES OR VARIETY | GROUP 1 | GROUP 2 | GROUP 3 |
|---|---|---|---|
| 'Jackmanii Alba'* | | ◆ | |
| 'John Warren' | | ◆ | |
| 'Lady Betty Balfour' | | | ◆ |
| 'Lasurstern' | | ◆ | |
| 'Lincoln Star' | | ◆ | |
| C. macropetala and cultivars | ◆ | | |
| 'Mme Edouard André' | | | ◆ |
| 'Marie Boisselot' | | ◆ | |
| 'Miss Bateman' | | ◆ | |
| C. montana and cultivars | ◆ | | |
| 'Mrs Cholmondeley' | | ◆ | |
| 'Nelly Moser' | | ◆ | |
| 'Niobe' | | ◆ | |
| 'Proteus'* | | ◆ | |
| 'Purpurea Plena Elegans' | | | ◆ |
| C. recta and cultivars | | | ◆ |
| C. rehderiana | | | ◆ |
| 'Rouge Cardinal' | | | ◆ |
| 'Royal Velvet' | | ◆ | |
| 'Silver Moon' | | ◆ | |
| 'Star of India' | | | ◆ |
| 'Sylvia Denny' | | ◆ | |
| C. tangutica and cultivars | | | ◆ |
| 'The President' | | ◆ | |
| 'Venosa Violacea' | | | ◆ |
| 'Ville de Lyon' | | | ◆ |
| 'Vyvyan Pennell' | | ◆ | |

## Renovation

Rampant Group 1 clematis, such as C. montana and C. armandii, can become very congested and woody, with only the topmost growth bearing flowers. To rejuvenate the plant, immediately after flowering cut back all growth into the woody framework, if necessary to within 1–2m (3¼–6½ft) of the base. Feed the plant with a general fertilizer, water well and apply a mulch to conserve moisture.

Plants recover quickly and will start to shoot again within a few weeks. Clematis may not flower the first year after renovative pruning.

# Propagation

Clematis can be propagated in a
variety of ways. Species, such as
*C. tangutica* and *C. rehderiana*, can
be raised from seed. Seed gathered
from cultivars of species, such as
*C. montana* 'Elizabeth', will revert to
type – the resultant plants will not, or
are unlikely to, inherit the distinguish-
ing features of the cultivar. Hybrids
may set seed, but any plants raised
from it will not be similar to the
parent, and seldom make good garden
plants. They have to be increased by
vegetative methods as detailed below.

## Propagating by layering

This is usually a highly successful
method, since the new plant remains
connected to the parent until it has
rooted. However, it is not usually
practical to raise more than a couple
of new plants per year from each
parent using this method.

A variation on this technique that
will produce more plants is serpentine
layering. The stem is wounded
between each (or every other) node,
and is pegged directly to the soil at
each of these points with pieces of
wire bent into a U shape.

2 Dab hormone rooting powder into the
cut with a soft paintbrush.

1 (*left*) In early spring, select a strong,
non-flowering shoot from near the
base of the plant. Prepare a pot
containing equal parts of peat and sharp
sand. (Do not use lightweight perlite,
since the pot needs to be as stable as
possible.) Midway between two leaf joints,
about 30cm (1ft) along the stem, cut a
tongue in the wood on the underside of
the stem using a sharp knife.

3 Bring the cut section of the stem into
contact with the rooting medium, and
peg down the stem with a piece of wire
bent into a U shape.

4 Insert a thin cane into the side of the
pot. Tie the stem loosely to the cane,
either with a wire tie bent into a figure of
eight or a length of horticultural string.
The layer should take about a year to root,
after which you can sever it from the
parent. Repot it into a loam-based
compost (soil mix) and grow it on,
planting it into its final position after
another year or two.

## TAKING INTERNODAL CUTTINGS

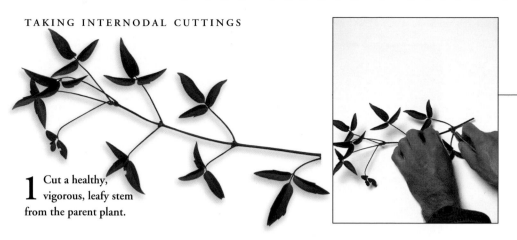

**1** Cut a healthy, vigorous, leafy stem from the parent plant.

**2** Cut the stem into one node (i.e. one leaf pair) sections. Each cutting should retain about 2.5cm (1in) of stem below the node, and a small piece just above.

**3** To accommodate several cuttings, cut off one of the pair of leaves.

**4** Dip the cutting in copper fungicide. Dip the base of the cutting in hormone rooting powder and tap off any excess.

**5** Insert the cutting in a pot containing equal parts of peat and perlite (or horticultural sand).

## Cuttings

Clematis can be propagated by cuttings taken in spring (softwood) or early summer (semi-ripe). You can take the cuttings in the conventional way, but a more effective method that is also more economical with plant material is by "internodal" cuttings. The stems are cut midway between nodes (leaf joints) and each stem will yield several cuttings. Place the prepared cuttings in a propagator and keep them in a semi-shaded position. Bottom heat will speed up rooting but is not essential.

**6** Spray the cuttings with fungicide to kill off any fungal spores. Insert the pots into a propagator, placed out of direct sunlight. The cuttings should root in 6–8 weeks. Pot them up individually and harden off gradually. In cold areas, overwinter the young plants in a cold frame. Grow them on for at least a year before planting them out.

PROPAGATING BY DIVISION

## Propagating herbaceous clematis

Herbaceous clematis can be divided in late winter or spring as new growth is emerging. Use this method both to increase your stock and to thin congested plants. Spare divisions can be composted, replanted elsewhere in the garden, or given to friends. Species can also be propagated from seed (see opposite).

Alternatively, propagate herbaceous clematis by basal cuttings taken in early spring. Select a sturdy shoot and cut it off at ground level, making sure that the base of the cutting retains a small piece of the plant's woody crown. Remove any lower leaves and dab the base with hormone rooting powder. Then insert the cuttings into pots containing a rooting medium of equal parts peat and horticultural sand (or perlite). Spray the cuttings with a fungicidal solution in order to kill any bacteria.

Place the pots in a propagator or put them inside a plastic bag which acts as a tent. The cuttings should root after 4–6 weeks, after which they can be potted up individually and grown on for about a year before planting out.

**1** When new growth emerges, cut off any dead growth.

**2** Dig up the clump with a fork and shake the rootball free of excess soil.

**3** Tease the clump apart with your hands, using a handfork if necessary. With an old, congested clump, you may need to prise the plant apart with two garden forks placed back to back. Each section should have a good root system and strong new shoots.

**4** Replace the best pieces, either *in situ* or in another part of the garden. Discard any pieces that are very woody, or that carry a high proportion of dead growth.

---

### HERBACEOUS CLEMATIS THAT MAY BE DIVIDED OR INCREASED BY BASAL CUTTINGS

*C.* x *durandii* and cultivars

*C. heracleifolia* and cultivars

*C. integrifolia* and cultivars

*C. recta* and cultivars

## (Propagation by seed

All clematis species can be propagated by seed. You can gather your own by pulling the fluffy seed away from the seedhead when ripe (this is usually in autumn), but seed is also available commercially. Any seed that you gather yourself is best sown immediately and is usually quick to germinate. Stored or bought seed sown in autumn will germinate the following spring.

Sow the seed thinly in seed trays or pots, using a good proprietary seed

### WHICH CLEMATIS TO GROW FROM SEED

| |
|---|
| C. alpina |
| C. armandii |
| C. campaniflora |
| C. cirrhosa |
| C. flammula |
| C. integrifolia |
| C. macropetala |
| C. montana |
| C. recta |
| C. tangutica |
| C. terniflora |
| C. texensis |
| C. tibetana |
| C. viorna |
| C. viticella |

### SOWING SEED

**1** Cover the holes at the base of the pot or seed tray with crocks or stones to improve drainage.

**2** Fill the pot with a mixture of two parts seed compost (potting soil) to one part horticultural grit. Firm the compost (potting soil), and moisten it by standing it in a tray of water.

**3** Sow the seed thinly on the surface of the compost (potting soil).

**4** Cover the seed with a thin layer of horticultural grit. Label the pots, then place them in a cold frame outdoors to overwinter.

compost (potting soil) with added grit for improved drainage. Once the seedlings are large enough to handle (generally when two sets of true leaves have developed), prick them out into individual pots of potting compost (potting soil). Grow the seedlings on in a cold frame until they are large enough to plant out in their final positions, usually after a year.

# Pests and diseases

Clematis that have been correctly planted, and that are well fed, receiving adequate moisture, are generally very healthy plants that are not prone to pests and diseases.

Throughout the growing season, check for any dead or damaged growth on the plants, and cut it back to healthy wood immediately. All plant material showing

## Aphids

*How to identify:* The pest clusters around the shoot tips or beneath young leaves in late spring and early summer,

## Mice and voles

*How to identify:* The young shoots are eaten as they emerge from around the base of the plants.

A ladybird feeding on pests.

A hoverfly eating pests.

Aphids (greenfly).

Also, many weaker-growing cultivars have been lost to cultivation, being replaced by stronger ones, so that clematis wilt, once the scourge of clematis growers, has become a less common problem.

Maintaining good garden hygiene considerably reduces any risk of serious damage to plants. In autumn, clear away any dead leaves that accumulate around the base of the plants. Rotting vegetation can encourage bacteria and fungi to multiply, while harbouring overwintering pests and their eggs.

signs of disease should be burnt and not composted, since this could reintroduce harmful organisms into the soil. Also note that systemic sprays do not kill pests directly; they are absorbed by the plant and poison the pests when plant tissue is ingested. Since the effect is not immediate, repeated applications are usually necessary. When using any fungicide or insecticide, always follow the manufacturer's instructions.

The following are some of the problems you may encounter in the garden.

causing the leaves to curl downwards.
*Control:* Spray with a proprietary systemic insecticide, repeating as directed by the manufacturer. Some insecticides are selective in their action and leave beneficial insects such as ladybirds unharmed. Organic insecticides are also available.
*Prevention:* This is not usually possible. Aphids are endemic in virtually every garden, though their prevalence varies from year to year depending on the severity of the previous winter.

*Control:* Set traps (humane or otherwise) or poisoned baits from late winter onwards, then protect the shoots with pipes as detailed below.
*Prevention:* The simplest and most humane method to prevent mice and voles damaging clematis is to protect the emerging shoots with a 30cm (1ft) length of land drain or piping. This need not be unsightly if the clematis is growing among other plants that will conceal it. The pipe can be removed once the growth is firm and less palatable to the pests.

## Earwigs

*How to identify:* Leaves and flowers are partly eaten; flower damage is particularly likely late in the season.

**Earwig damage.**

*Control:* Since the insects hide during the day and are active at night, picking them off by hand is unlikely to be feasible. Set traps – either position half a grapefruit rind at the base of the plant, or stuff a flowerpot with straw (see Calendar) and invert it on a cane, inserted in the ground. Each morning dispose of earwigs that congregate in the trap. Alternatively, spray with a recommen ded proprietary insecticide. The best time to spray is at dusk.
*Prevention:* Not usually possible.

## Slugs and snails

*How to identify:* Emerging shoots and leaves are eaten. Silvery trails around the plant indicate their presence.

*Control:* Apply slug pellets around the base of the plant in early spring, before mulching. As they are effective in wet weather only, several applications may be necessary. You can also use a parasitic nematode applied as a root drench in late winter.
*Prevention:* Clear away any plant debris around the plant that may provide a nesting site in autumn. Remove large stones from the vicinity that may also harbour the pests. With container-grown clematis regularly check the undersides of the containers.

## Mildew

*How to identify:* A greyish powdering on leaves, usually in late summer; in severe cases it covers the whole plant.

**Mildew.**

*Cause:* Various fungi that thrive in dry soils. Mildew is most likely to affect wall-trained clematis: the soil is probably dry, and the circulation of air through the top-growth poor. Some cultivars are more prone to mildew than others.
*Control:* Spray with a proprietary fungicide and thin congested growth.
*Prevention:* Keep wall-trained clematis well-fed and watered in the growing season. Prune and train the shoots carefully to avoid congested growth.

## Wilt

*How to identify:* The top-growth blackens and dies back; unchecked, the whole plant dies back.

**Wilt.**

*Cause:* The fungal disease *Asochyta clamatidina.*
*Control:* None possible, once wilt has taken hold. If pruned hard, clematis that have been planted deeply enough usually recover.
*Prevention:* Drenching with fungicide at monthly intervals in the growing season may help, but if wilt is a persistent problem replace your clematis with others known to be less susceptible to the disease. Clematis species (apart from *C. montana*) and small-flowered hybrids are immune.

# Calendar

## Late winter

Prune clematis Groups 2 and 3. Divide herbaceous clematis if congested, and to increase your stock.

**When propagating by division, select sections that have a good root system.**

## Spring

Plant new stock. Mulch established plants. Prune Group 1 clematis after flowering, if necessary. Cut back newly planted clematis and others planted the previous year. To increase your stock, take basal cuttings of herbaceous clematis; layer or take softwood cuttings of climbers. Protect young shoots from slugs and snails with slug pellets, and from slugs alone by applying a parasitic nematode. Prevent mouse damage by protecting shoots with sections of land drain.

**Spring is the flowering time for Group 1 clematis, such as *C. montana*, shown here. After flowering, cut back any stems that have outgrown their space.**

Treat plants that may be susceptible to mildew. Spray against greenfly. Treat the soil with fungicide where wilt is likely to be a problem.

**In summer stuff pots with straw to make earwig traps.**

## Summer

Plant new stock, in suitable conditions. Take semi-ripe cuttings to increase your stock. Set earwig traps to control the pest. Continue to spray mildewed plants with a fungicide and thin the top-growth. Continue to treat the soil with fungicide where wilt is a problem.

**Mulching adds nutrients to the soil and helps prevent loss of moisture.**

## Autumn

Plant new stock of hardy types. Fork in bonemeal around the base of established plants, then mulch. Cut back overlong stems on Group 1 clematis (optional). Sow seed of species clematis.

# Other recommended clematis

Heights and spreads, given at the end of the description, are approximate and will vary according to the local climate, soil type and season. Flowering times may also vary from year to year.

*C. aethusifolia* (Group 3). Herbaceous species clematis with erect or scandent stems that carry bell-shaped, pale yellow to creamy-white flowers in summer. 60cm (2ft) x 60cm (2ft).

'Alba Luxurians' (Group 3). Viticella-type clematis with half-nodding, green-tipped, single white flowers in profusion from mid- to late summer. 4m (13ft) x 1.5m (5ft).

'Alba Luxurians'.

*C. alpina* (Group 1). Species clematis with nodding, bell-shaped, blue flowers from spring to early summer. 3m (10ft) x 1.5m (5ft). Cultivars include 'Frances Rivis', with paler flowers, and

*C. alpina.*

'Helsinborg', with purple-blue flowers.

'Asao' (Group 2). Large-flowered clematis with single, warm pink flowers, the sepals edged with deeper pink, from late spring to summer. 2m (6¹/₂ft) x 90cm (3ft).

'Ascotiensis' (Group 3). Large-flowered clematis with large blue flowers in summer. 4m (13ft) x 90cm (3ft).

'Barbara Jackman' (Group 2). Large-flowered clematis with blue flowers barred with petunia pink from mid-summer to early autumn. 3m (10ft) x 90cm (3ft).

'Beauty of Worcester' (Group 2). Large-flowered clematis with deep blue flowers from late spring to mid-summer. The early flowers are double; summer flowers are single. 2.5m (8ft) x 90cm (3ft).

'Belle of Woking' (Group 2). Large-flowered clematis with double white flowers from late spring to late summer.

2.5m (8ft) x 90cm (3ft).

'Betty Corning' (Group 3). Viticella-type clematis with pale lilac flowers from mid-summer to late autumn. 2m (6¹/₂ft) x 90cm (3ft).

'Blue Gem' (Group 2). Large-flowered clematis with lavender-blue flowers throughout summer. 2m (6¹/₂ft) x 90cm (3ft).

*C. campaniflora* (Group 3). Species clematis with charming, hanging, bowl-shaped, white flowers that are tinged violet in summer. 6m (20ft) x 2m (6¹/₂ft).

'Captain Thuilleaux' (Group 2). Large-flowered clematis

'Comtesse de Bouchaud'.

with deep pink flowers from late spring to early summer. 2m (6¹/₂ft) x 90cm (3ft).

'Carnaby' (Group 2). Large-flowered clematis with deep pink flowers from late spring to early summer. 2.5m (8ft) x 90cm (3ft).

'Comtesse de Bouchaud' (Group 3). Large-flowered

clematis with mauve-pink flowers in late summer. 3m (10ft) x 90cm (3ft).

'Corona' (Group 2). Large-flowered clematis with purplish-pink flowers from late spring to early summer, and in late summer. 2m (6¹/₂ft) x 90cm (3ft).

'Countess of Lovelace' (Group 2). Large-flowered clematis with lilac-blue flowers from late spring to mid-summer; early flowers are double, late ones single. 2m (6¹/₂ft) x 90cm (3ft).

'Crimson King' (Group 3). Large-flowered clematis with crimson flowers from mid- to late summer. 2m (6¹/₂ft) x 90cm (3ft).

*C. crispa* (Group 3). Species clematis with lavender-blue, nodding, bell-shaped flowers in summer. 2.5m (8ft) x 90cm (3ft).

'Daniel Deronda' (Group 2). Large-flowered clematis with purple-blue flowers from late spring to late summer. Early flowers are double or semi-double; late ones are single. 2m (6¹/₂ft) x 90cm (3ft).

'Dr Ruppel' (Group 2). Large-flowered clematis with pink flowers barred with deeper pink from late spring to mid-summer. 2.5m (8ft) x 90cm (3ft).

'Duchess of Sutherland' (Group 2). Large-flowered clematis which bears carmine

'Etoile Violette'.

flowers from late spring to mid-summer. 2m (6½ft) x 90cm (3ft).

*C.* x *durandii* (Group 3). Hybrid, shrubby clematis with scandent stems that produces saucer-shaped, deep violet-blue flowers in summer-autumn. 90cm–2m (3–6½ft) x 90cm–2m (3–6½ft), depending on support.

'Elsa Späth' (Group 2). Large-flowered clematis with mid-blue flowers from late spring to late summer. 3m (10ft) x 90cm (3ft).

*C.* x *eriostemon* (Group 3). Hybrid, shrubby clematis with scandent stems that produces bell-shaped, deep violet flowers from mid- to late summer. 90cm–3m (3–10ft) x 90cm–3m (3–10ft), depending on support. 'Hendersonii' has violet-blue flowers on thicker stems.

'Ernest Markham' (Group 3). Large-flowered clematis with masses of magenta flowers from early to late summer. 4m (13ft) x 90cm (3ft).

'Etoile Rose' (Group 3). Texensis-type clematis with rose-red flowers in late summer. 2.5m (8ft) x 90cm (3ft).

'Etoile Violette' (Group 3). Viticella-type clematis with violet flowers from mid-summer to early autumn. 5m (17ft) x 1.5m (5ft).

'Fair Rosamund' (Group 2). Large-flowered clematis with white flowers barred with pink in late spring and early summer. 2m (6½ft) x 90cm (3ft).

*C. florida* 'Sieboldii' (Group 2). Large-flowered clematis with passion flower-like white flowers with purple centres from mid-summer to early autumn. 2m (6½ft) x 90cm (3ft).

'General Sikorski' (Group 2). Large-flowered clematis with mid-blue, single flowers in mid-summer. 3m (10ft) x 90cm (3ft).

'Gipsy Queen' (Group 3). Large-flowered clematis with violet-purple flowers in late summer. 3m (10ft) x 90cm (3ft).

'Guernsey Cream' (Group 2). Large-flowered clematis with creamy-white flowers in late spring and early summer. 2m (6½ft) x 90cm (3ft).

'Hagley Hybrid' (Group 3). Large-flowered clematis with pinkish-mauve flowers from early to late summer. 2m (6½ft) x 90cm (3ft).

'Haku Okan' (Group 2). Large-flowered clematis with rich violet flowers in late spring and early summer and again in late summer. 2m (6½ft) x 90cm (3ft).

'Henryi' (Group 2). Large-flowered clematis with creamy-white flowers from early to late summer. 2m (6½ft) x 90cm (3ft).

'H.F. Young' (Group 2). Large-flowered clematis with violet-tinged blue flowers from late spring to early summer. 2.5m (8ft) x 90cm (3ft).

'Horn of Plenty' (Group 2). Large-flowered clematis with lilac-mauve flowers with red anthers in early summer. 2.5m (8ft) x 90cm (3ft).

*C. integrifolia* (Group 3).

'John Huxtable'.

Herbaceous, sub-shrubby clematis with narrow to broad bell-shaped, deep violet or blue (sometimes white) flowers in summer. 60cm (2ft) x 60cm (2ft).

'Jackmanii' (Group 3). Large-flowered clematis with rich purple flowers from mid- to late summer. 3m (10ft) x 90cm (3ft).

*C. montana* f. *grandiflora*.

'Jackmanii Alba' (Group 2). Large-flowered clematis with white flowers from early to late summer. Early flowers are double; later ones are single. 3m (10ft) x 90cm (3ft).

'Joan Picton' (Group 2). Large-flowered clematis with silver-lilac flowers in late spring and again in late summer. 2m (6½ft) x 90cm (3ft).

'John Huxtable' (Group 3). Large-flowered clematis with white flowers with cream anthers in mid-summer. 3m (10ft) x 90cm (3ft).

'John Paul II' (Group 2). Large-flowered clematis with pale pink flowers barred with deeper pink in summer.

2m (6¹/₂ft) x 90cm (3ft).
**'Kardynal Wyszynski'**
(Group 3). Large-flowered clematis with crimson flowers in mid- to late summer. 3m (10ft) x 90cm (3ft).
**'Kathleen Dunford'** (Group 2). Large-flowered clematis with deep lavender-pink flowers throughout summer. 2m (6¹/₂ft) x 90cm (3ft).
**'Lady Betty Balfour'** (Group 3). Large-flowered clematis with purple flowers in late summer to early autumn. 3m (10ft) x 90cm (3ft).

*C. montana* 'Marjorie'.

**'Lady Caroline Nevill'** (Group 2). Large-flowered clematis with bluish-mauve flowers in late spring and again in late summer. Early flowers are semi-double; later ones are single. 2m (6¹/₂ft) x 90cm (3ft).
**'Lincoln Star'** (Group 2). Large-flowered clematis with raspberry-pink flowers from late spring to early summer. 2.5m (8ft) x 90cm (3ft).

**'Lord Nevill'** (Group 2). Large-flowered clematis with deep blue flowers throughout the summer. 2m (6¹/₂ft) x 90cm (3ft).
*C. macropetala* (Group 1). Species clematis with nodding, apparently double, bell-shaped blue or violet-blue flowers in mid- to late spring. 3m (10ft) x 1.5m (5ft). Cultivars include: **'Bluebird'** (mid-blue flowers); **'Markham's Pink'** (strawberry-pink); and **'White Moth'** (white).
**'Mme Edouard André'** (Group 3). Large-flowered clematis with deep red flowers in summer. 2.5m (8ft) x 90cm (3ft).
**'Mme Grangé'** (Group 3). Large-flowered clematis with reddish-purple flowers in late summer. 3m (10ft) x 90cm (3ft).
**'Mme Julia Correvon'** (Group 3). Viticella-type clematis with ruby-red flowers from mid-summer through to early autumn. 3m (10ft) x 1.5m (5ft).
**'Maureen'** (Group 2). Large-flowered clematis with rich purple flowers throughout the summer. 2m (6¹/₂ft) x 90cm (3ft).
**'Minuet'** (Group 3). Viticella-type clematis with white flowers edged with mauve in late summer. 3m (10ft) x 90cm (3ft).

*C. montana* 'Tetrarose'.

**'Miss Bateman'** (Group 2). Large-flowered clematis with creamy-white flowers in late spring to early summer. 2.5m (8ft) x 90cm (3ft).
*C. montana* (Group 1). Species clematis with saucer-shaped, white flowers in late spring. 5–8m (17–26ft) x 3m (10ft). Cultivars and forms include: **'Elizabeth'** (pale pink flowers); f. *grandiflora* (white; very vigorous); **'Marjorie'** (creamy-pink, tinted orange); **'Tetrarose'** (rich pink; the leaves are tinged bronze); and **var.** *wilsonii* (fragrant, white, profuse).
**'Mrs N. Thompson'** (Group 2). Large-flowered clematis with purplish-blue flowers barred with petunia-pink throughout summer. 2m (6¹/₂ft) x 90cm (3ft).
**'Mrs Spencer Castle'** (Group 2). Large-flowered clematis with mauve-pink flowers in late spring and in late summer. Early flowers are

double; later ones are single. 2m (6¹/₂ft) x 90cm (3ft).
**'Niobe'** (Group 2). Large-flowered clematis with deep red flowers throughout summer. 3m (10ft) x 90cm (3ft).
**'Perle d'Azur'** (Group 3). Large-flowered clematis with azure-blue flowers from mid-summer to early autumn. 3m (10ft) x 90cm (3ft).
*C. petriei* (Group 3). Species clematis with yellowish-green flowers in summer to autumn. 4m (13ft) x 2m (6¹/₂ft). Cultivars include **'Limelight'**, with lime-green flowers and purplish foliage.
**'Pink Fantasy'** (Group 3). Large-flowered clematis with pale pink flowers barred with

*C. montana* 'Wilsonii'.

deeper pink from mid-through to late summer. 3m (10ft) x 90cm (3ft).
**'Polish Spirit'** (Group 3). Viticella-type clematis with rich purple flowers from mid-summer to late autumn. 5m (15ft) x 2m (6¹/₂ft).

'The President'.

'**Proteus**' (Group 2). Large-flowered clematis with mauve-pink flowers in late spring and early summer, repeating in late summer. Early flowers are double; the late flowers are single, paler and smaller. 3m (10ft) x 90cm (3ft).

'**Ramona**' (Group 2). Large-flowered clematis with pale blue flowers from mid-summer to autumn. 3m (10ft) x 90cm (3ft).

*C. recta* (Group 3). Herbaceous species clematis with star-shaped, fragrant, milk-white flowers from mid-summer to autumn. 1.5m (5ft) x 75cm (2¹/₂ft).

'**Richard Pennell**' (Group 2). Large-flowered clematis with deep plum-purple flowers from late spring to mid-summer. 3m (10ft) x 90cm (3ft).

'**Sealander Gem**' (Group 2). Large-flowered clematis with pinkish-mauve flowers barred with deeper pink in late spring and early summer. 2m (6¹/₂ft) x 90cm (3ft).

'**Snow Queen**' (Group 2). Large-flowered clematis with blue-tinged, white flowers in late spring, repeating in late summer to early autumn. 2.5m (8ft) x 90cm (3ft).

'**Star of India**' (Group 3). Large-flowered clematis with deep purple-blue flowers barred with carmine-red in mid-summer. 3m (10ft) x 90cm (3ft).

'**Sunset**' (Group 3). Large-flowered clematis with red flowers in mid-summer. 2.5m (8ft) x 90cm (3ft).

'**Sylvia Denny**' (Group 2). Large-flowered clematis with white flowers in early summer, repeating in late summer. The early flowers are double and the later ones are single and smaller. 2.5m (8ft) x 90cm (3ft).

*C. recta.*

*C. terniflora* (Group 3). Species clematis with star-shaped, white flowers in late summer to early autumn. 5m (15ft) x 3m (10ft).

*C. tibetana* ssp. *vernayi* (Group 3). Species clematis with lantern-like, greenish-yellow to burnt orange flowers in mid-summer. 6m (20ft) x 2m (6¹/₂ft).

'**The President**' (Group 2). Large-flowered clematis with rich purple flowers from late spring to early autumn. 3m (10ft) x 90cm (3ft).

'**Twilight**' (Group 3). Large-flowered clematis with magenta-red to mauve flowers from mid-summer to early autumn. 3m (10ft) x 90cm (3ft).

'**Venosa Violacea**' (Group 3). Viticella-type clematis with white flowers, veined purple, from mid- to late summer. 3m (10ft) x 90cm (3ft).

'**Vino**' (Group 2). Large-flowered clematis with purple-red flowers in early summer. 3m (10ft) x 90cm (3ft).

*C. viorna* (Group 1). Shrubby species clematis with scandent stems that carry nodding urn-shaped, violet or dull purple flowers in spring to summer. To 3m (10ft) x 2m (6¹/₂ft) if supported.

*C. vitalba* (Group 3). Species clematis with panicles of small, greenish-white flowers in summer, followed by fluffy grey seedheads. 30m (100ft) x 10m (33ft).

'**Vyvyan Pennell**' (Group 2). Large-flowered clematis with rich lilac-blue flowers from late spring to late summer. Early flowers are double; later ones are single. 3m (10ft) x 90cm (3ft).

'**Wada's Primrose**' (Group 2). Large-flowered clematis with creamy-white flowers in late spring to early summer. 2.5m (8ft) x 90cm (3ft).

'**Walter Pennell**' (Group 2). Large-flowered clematis with

*C. viorna.*

deep lilac flowers barred with carmine-pink in late spring and early summer. 2m (6¹/₂ft) x 90cm (3ft).

'**W.E. Gladstone**' (Group 2). Large-flowered clematis with lavender-blue flowers from late spring to late summer. 3m (10ft) x 90cm (3ft).

'**Will Godwin**' (Group 2). Large-flowered clematis with lavender flowers from early to late summer. 2m (6¹/₂ft) x 90cm (3ft).

'**William Kennett**' (Group 2). Large-flowered clematis with pale lavender-blue flowers in summer. 3m (10ft) x 90cm (3ft).

# Index

## ACKNOWLEDGEMENTS

The publishers would like to thank the following people for allowing photography of their gardens: Christopher Lloyd, Great Dixter, E. Sussex; J.F. and L.F. Arbuthnott, Stone House Cottage Nurseries, Worcs; Miss R. Cole, Mrs A. Hartley and Mrs S. Allen of Long Buckby, Northants; The Hon. and Mrs Simon Howard, Castle Howard, Yorks; Treasures of Tenbury, Burford House, Tenbury Wells, Worcs. They would also like to thank the following people for allowing reproduction of their photographs: The Harry Smith Collection, 2, 12t, 44, 45, 56r and 64; Christopher Grey-Wilson, 9b, 11, 25tr, 27b and 35b; the Harpur Garden Picture Library, 10 and 18b (Helmingham Hall); Peter McHoy, 19b, 34m, 49, 56l, 56m, 59m, 59r, 60l–r, 61m and 61r; the Garden Picture Library, 43b, and the author, 18t and 61l.